Grief: The Event, The Work, The Forever

A self-help book brought to you by the letter "R"

Lisa Zoll, LCSW
Lynn Shiner

You can find us on Facebook with our logo – Search "A Grief Trajectory." Like us. Follow us. Share posts that might be helpful to anyone who is grieving.

The content in Grief: The Event, The Work, The Forever is for informational purposes only and not intended as a substitute for professional advice, counseling or treatment.

Dedication

This book is dedicated with love to the memory of Lynn's children, Jen and Dave, and Lisa's parents, K. Richard and Yvonne B. Shaull, and her nephew, Abe Jacobs.

Acknowledgments

Our sincere appreciation to the individuals who have creatively and graciously contributed their talents to helping make this book more meaningful through their illustrations: Zaili Schwartzman, Lorie Shaull (Lisa's sister – through the Noun Project and photos), Jen & Dave (Lynn's children), Abe Jacobs (Lisa's nephew), Charley Washinger, Natalie Novotny-Goles, Shannon Wood, Nicole Shiner, Jenna Mortimer, Bonnie Spease Bentz, Kelsey Bentz, Linda Jacobs, Leigh Ann Bryan, Bob Monk, Michelle Smey, and Shannon O'Shea.

Our thanks to Chick Zoll and Paul Shiner for their support of this project.

Thanks to Matt Cleckner for developing the logo (AGT) and Facebook page (A Grief Trajectory) for this project.

Our appreciation to Nancy Eshelman for her expertise in proofreading and editing this project.

Thanks, gratitude, and appreciation to our friends and colleagues who took time to read over our manuscripts and provided valuable feedback to help get this book ready for publication. Thanks to James Corbin, LSW, Linda Jacobs, RN, The Rev. Dianne Andrews, Amy Boeshore, Ed Katz, and Mark, Erin, Nick, and Nina Bellusci.

Contents

Introduction

There's a very simple saying that there are only two things we have to do in our lifetime: pay taxes and die. We are all pretty good at talking and complaining about taxes, but those same voices are often muted when it comes to death, its impact, how we grieve, how it affects relationships, or how we celebrate a life that has been lost.

Lynn Shiner's children, Jen and Dave, 10 and 8, were stabbed to death by their father on Christmas Day 1994. Lynn subsequently co-authored an award-winning book entitled *Stabbed in the Heart: Three Murdered Children, Two Resilient Mothers.*

Lisa Zoll is a Licensed Clinical Social Worker who has taught classes on Loss and Grief at Temple University in its Master of Social Work program in Harrisburg and Philadelphia since 2008. She has experienced a number of losses, including her parents, close friends, and a nephew who died tragically in a car accident at the age of 23.

Together, they wanted to develop a tool that would not only benefit the griever, but the griever's support system as well. This includes family, friends, co-workers, clergy, victim advocates, social workers, counselors, psychologists, and any other person(s) who will be touched by the death.

This book is divided into four parts:

Part I – An Introduction to Grief: What grief is and some of the common physical, emotional, cognitive, behavioral, and spiritual responses to grief.

Part II – A Grief Trajectory: A realistic approach to the journey of grief that includes: The Event, the reaction; The

Working Grief, the reconstruction; and The Forever Grief, the remembering. This new model has eliminated stages, expectations, tasks, timelines, and the expectation of closure.

Part III – The "R" Words: An interactive exercise that allows grievers to select a word and apply it to any part of their grief journey. Talking about the event, the feelings, the loss, the present, and the future is a critical part of the grieving process.

Part IV – Supporting the Griever: Suggestions on how to interact and support the griever.

Appendix – Contains the published article "A Grief Trajectory" that the concepts in this book are based upon.

Grief is complex, and everyone's journey is unique. It is our hope that this book lays a foundation to help grievers understand common reactions to their loss(es), validate their grief responses, encourage the telling of their story, and provide supportive advice to family and friends.

This book is intended to be a resource for grievers and their support systems. Professional help is always recommended if the responses to the loss(es) become overwhelming or unbearable.

"Grief is the scholar of life. Its teachings are immeasurable. It is a powerful reminder of how fragile life can be."(Lynn Shiner)

Part I:
An Introduction
to Grief

Photo Credit: Lynn Shiner

What is the first thing you think of when you hear the word *grief*?

Words you might hear...

agony, anguish, painful, eternal, lonely, forever, excruciating, infinite, nightmare, empty, unbearable, broken, determined, overwhelming, wordless, lost, random, shattered, constant, indescribable, unwanted, unexplainable, unreal, piercing, unimaginable, ache, sucks, destroyed, devastating, crushing, longing, desperate, all-consuming, life-long, endless, lifetime, hell, crippling, roller-coaster, unforgiving, relentless, void, murder, torture, dead, powerful, exhausting, unending, unbelievable, sorrow, unreal, catastrophic, daunting, joylessness, enlightening, lifeless, numbing, unendurable, draining, consuming, horrendous, hollow, disorienting, surreal, misery, inconsistent, sad, lingering, depressed, always, everlasting, encompassing, breathtaking, despair, heavy, tearful, bad, eviscerating, horror, intense, changed, hideous, anger, brave, scared, melancholy, gut-wrenching, unfathomable, everyday, terminal, necessary, stages, healing, ongoing, life-changing and amputation

There are an endless number of words that can be used to describe a person's grief. Have you used or heard others use these words as they talk about their grief? Do any of these fit into your experience(s) of grief? Are there other words you would use?

_____

_____

_____

_____

_____

_____

_____

_____

_____

Grief is the physical, emotional, cognitive, behavioral, and spiritual response to the loss of someone, somewhere, or something to which a significant emotional bond has been formed.

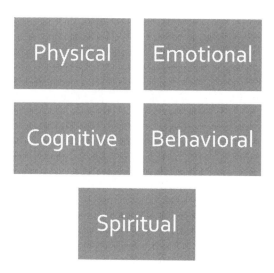

The Uncommon becomes Common
The Atypical becomes Typical

Responses to Grief:
Physical

Upset stomach, lack of energy, muscle weakness, changes in sleep patterns, changes in appetite, heaviness on the chest, oversensitivity to noise, numbness, sense of the presence of the deceased...

Responses to Grief:
Emotional

Anger, sadness, shock, anxiety, guilt, denial, emptiness, relief, depression, panic, fear, helplessness, loneliness, apathy, numbness...

Responses to Grief:
Cognitive

Disbelief, preoccupation about the deceased, yearning, confusion, difficulty concentrating, short-term memory loss, vivid dreams about the deceased...

Responses to Grief:
Behavioral

Social withdrawal and isolation, absentminded behavior, loss of interest in the outside world, searching and calling out, sighing, restlessness, hyperactivity, treasuring objects of the deceased...

Responses to Grief:
Spiritual

Blaming God, lack of direction and hope, wishing to join the person who has died, lack of purpose, questioning the meaning of life...

Exercise:
Multifaceted Responses to Grief

In this exercise, take time to reflect on your physical, emotional, cognitive, behavioral, and spiritual responses to the event(s) that you have experienced.

Physical

1. What physical reactions have you had in response to the loss(es)?

2. What physical responses seemed to linger for the longest time?

3. What kind of activities have you stopped doing that you liked to do before the event? Is there something keeping you from doing them?

Emotional

1. Has it been difficult to describe or explain your emotions/feelings to others? Why?

2. What have been some of the most helpful words or actions that others have offered you?

3. What have been least helpful?

Cognitive

1. Are your current memories of the deceased painful? Are they comforting? Are they both?

2. What are some of the most distressing thoughts you have experienced?

3. What do you worry about the most?

Behavioral

1. What activities have you identified that have been helpful to your grieving process?

2. How about unhelpful activities?

3. Have you found yourself behaving in ways that are not common for you?

4. How have you experienced the behaviors of others toward you?

Spiritual

1.   Have you asked "Why would God allow something like this to occur?"

2.   How has the loss impacted your religious and/or spiritual beliefs?

3.   Do you blame God, yourself, or someone else?

4.   Have you identified passages of scriptures, prayers, quotations, or sayings that are helpful or comforting to you?

Please Note: There is a wide range of responses to any grief event. Each experience is unique in its own way, and each response, (i.e. physical, emotional, cognitive, behavioral, or spiritual) is a way grief may be experienced. For example, an individual may experience emotional responses and not physical or behavioral ones. There is no one best response. There are simply different ways to respond to grief.

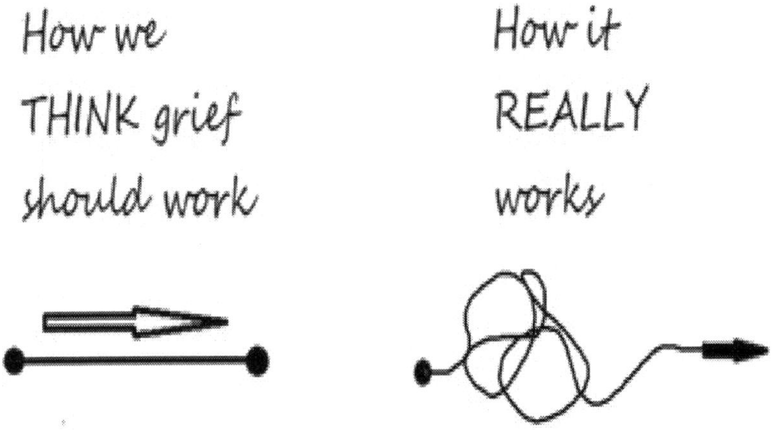

How we
THINK grief
should work

How it
REALLY
works

How does your grief work?
Draw your own perspective on
this page.

Notes and Reflections

_____

_____

_____

_____

_____

_____

_____

_____

_____

_____

_____

_____

_____

Part II:

A Grief

Trajectory

After the murders of Jen and
Dave, Lynn found it difficult to
place herself in any stage of grief,
to find any form of closure as it
related to the loss of her children,
or to fit her experience into any
model that was presented to her
in her grief counseling. Lynn feels
that she was not meeting the
expectations of the parameters
set by clinical models, which
resulted in additional feelings of
anxiety and inadequacy. In
hindsight, Lynn feels that her

experience could best be expressed in a trajectory: the event, the work, and the never-ending process of grieving the loss, the forever grief. Doing so removes stages, expectations, expected order of stages, time frames, and closure. The wheel depicts the non-linear nature of the grief process.

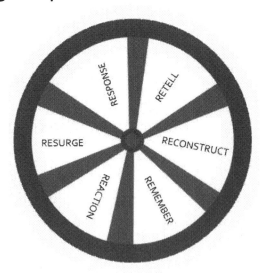

Any reference to time or a time frame has been purposefully omitted from the "event," "work," and "forever"process of the grief journey.

Time frames often reflect the wishes and discomfort of those witnessing an individual's grief, rather than the natural process of grief itself.

STUG = Resurge

Sudden Temporary Upsurges of Grief (STUG) – These events produce a reaction with periods of intense grief, which occur when a catalyst reminds one of the absence of the loved one, or resurrects memories of the death of a loved one, or feelings about the loss. (Rando, 1993)

STUG Reactions

These reactions can be expected and can happen in response to anniversaries, birthdays, and family celebrations.

Or they can be unexpected in the form of a song on the radio, a smell, or something that is read or seen that brings up a memory of the loss.

They tend to catch the individual off guard. (Rando, 1993)

What are some ways that you have been "STUG-ed" in your grief journey?

_____

_____

_____

_____

_____

_____

_____

_____

_____

_____

_____

_____

A Melting Pot of Emotions

A wide variety and combination of reactions and responses occur during the grieving process. The intensity, frequency, and duration of these tend to vary across the process and from person to person. Therefore, each griever's melting pot may be filled with different reactions and responses. During **"event grief,"** the pot may begin to fill with some overwhelming and very painful responses to the loss(es). During **"working grief,"** these responses can vary in their intensity, and can feel like they become heated to a boil in the pot. In general, these reactions tend to diminish in their intensity, frequency, and duration the further the griever moves within the process. Nevertheless, the responses can remain simmering in the pot indefinitely as indicated by **"forever grief."**

In the next few pages, some common responses to "**event grief**," "**working grief**," and "**forever grief**" are listed in no particular order. Circle the responses that you have experienced, cross out the ones that you have not, and add any additional responses that are not included in these lists. Note that these lists are not meant to be exhaustive, and responses will vary with each person's experience. While difficult to endure, many of the responses in the lists are not uncommon to the grieving process.

EVENT GRIEF = REACTION

The event that causes an individual to have a reaction to a loss.

These may include, but are not limited to, a tragic or unexpected death, a divorce, the loss of a job, or a move from a beloved home.

A Melting Pot of Emotions:
Common Grief Responses
in Event Grief

Suicidal thoughts
Numbness
Wailing
Vomiting
Bargaining
Racing heart
Chest pains
Deep sadness
Anger
Loss of control of daily life
Uncontrollable shaking
Shortness of breath
Guilt
Weakness in muscles
Searching behavior
Restlessness
Denial
Sobbing
Loss of appetite
Problems sleeping
Inability to concentrate
Shock

WORKING GRIEF = RECONSTRUCTION

Working grief is an engaging and ongoing process in which the griever defines the work that leads to some level of adaptation to the loss.

"When you can't go back, you have to worry only about the best way of moving forward" (Coelho, 1993, p. 77).

A MELTING POT OF EMOTIONS: COMMON GRIEF RESPONSES IN WORKING GRIEF

PANIC ATTACKS
SADNESS
DEPRESSION
EXPERIENCING THE PAIN OF THE
GRIEF
LINKING OBJECTS
QUESTIONING GOD/SPIRITUALITY
MEANING-MAKING
KEEPING THE DECEASED IN YOUR LIFE
ADJUSTING TO THE ENVIRONMENT
FEAR
ANXIETY
CONFUSION
HOPELESSNESS
LOSS OF CONFIDENCE
LOSS OF SELF-ESTEEM
VULNERABLITY
DIFFICULTY IN DECISION MAKING
WHAT IFS
LOSS OF INDEPENDENCE
STUGS

FOREVER GRIEF = REMEMBERING

Grief that lingers long after the loss but that no longer consumes or controls the griever's life.

"Simply put: You love them forever. Why wouldn't you grieve them forever?" (Lynn Shiner)

A Melting Pot of Emotions: Common Grief Responses in Forever Grief

Panic attacks
Sadness
Depression
Experiencing the pain of the grief
Linking objects
Questioning God/Spirituality
Meaning-making
Keeping the deceased in your life
Adjusting to the environment
Fear
Anxiety
Confusion
Hopelessness
Loss of confidence
Loss of self-esteem
Vulnerability
Difficulty in decision making
What ifs
Loss of independence
STUGs

The Melting Pot Summary

Event Grief	WORKING GRIEF	Forever Grief
Suicidal thoughts	PANIC ATTACKS	Panic attacks
Numbness	SADNESS	Sadness
Wailing	DEPRESSION	Depression
Vomiting	EXPERIENCING THE PAIN OF	Experiencing the pain of
Bargaining	THE GRIEF	the grief
Racing heart	LINKING OBJECTS	Linking objects
Chest pains	QUESTIONING GOD/	Questioning
Deep sadness	SPIRITUALITY	God/Spirituality
Anger	MEANING-MAKING	Meaning-making
Loss of control of daily life	KEEPING THE DECEASED IN	Keeping the deceased in
Uncontrollable shaking	YOUR LIFE	your life
Shortness of breath	ADJUSTING TO THE	Adjusting to the
Guilt	ENVIRONMENT	environment
Weakness in muscles	FEAR	Fear
Searching behavior	ANXIETY	Anxiety
Restlessness	CONFUSION	Confusion
Denial	HOPELESSNESS	Hopelessness
Sobbing	LOSS OF CONFIDENCE	Loss of confidence
Loss of appetite	LOSS OF SELF-ESTEEM	Loss of self-esteem
Problems with sleeping	VULNERABLITY	Vulnerability
Inability to concentrate	DIFFICULTY IN DECISION	Difficulty in decision
Shock	MAKING	making
	WHAT IFS	What ifs
	LOSS OF INDEPENDENCE	Loss of independence
	STUGS	STUGs

*Please note that these lists are not exhaustive and will vary from person to person.

While the trajectory of grief does not offer exact stages for individuals to pass through or tasks for individuals to accomplish, it demonstrates a trajectory that individuals may experience following a grief event. It suggests that grieving a loss may never come to a definitive end, and that "closure" is a myth. It does not mean that an individual cannot and will not return to a meaningful life by finding ways to accept the reality of the loss and adjust to a "new normal." This trajectory can serve as a path that begins at the grief event and moves through the twists and turns of the grief experience.

Notes and Reflections

_____

_____

_____

_____

_____

_____

_____

_____

_____

_____

_____

_____

_____

_____

Part III:

The "R" Words

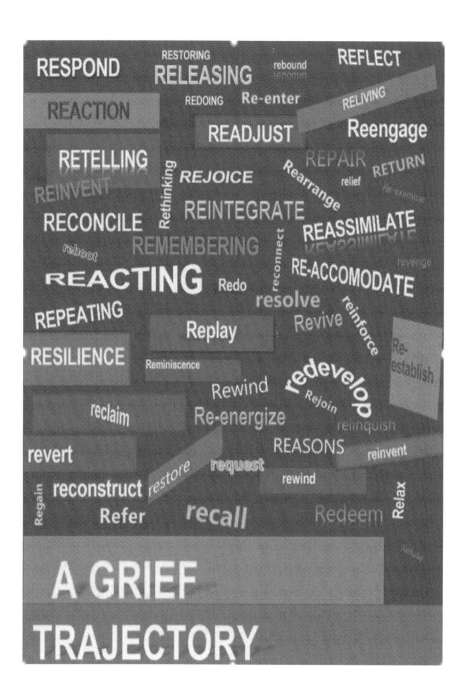

Charley W.

Sometimes, you just can't tell
anybody how you really feel.
Not because you don't know why,
not because you don't know
your purpose, not because you
don't trust them, but because
you can't find the right words to
make them understand.

~Unknown

The "R" Words

Each page of this part of the book contains an "R" ("re" to be exact) word that is a result of the grief trajectory. Each word can be applied to some aspect of the grief process.

When grievers tell their stories, they are often struggling to make sense of the event. Storytelling, and retelling, is an integral part of the grieving process. It can be an empowering way for grievers to find their voice in search of a way to accept the loss(es), and to cope with the subsequent responses that have left them feeling out of control and struggling with what has been stripped away from their life. Storytelling and retelling may also help to teach and guide the listener(s).

Open the book to any page in this section and find a way to relate the word on the page to any aspect of loss(es) that you have experienced.

The hope is that this book will be an aid in opening up about grief event(s) and the identifying grief work that you have done, although you may not realize it. Grievers are encouraged to be creative in applying the "R" words to their experience(s) of loss and grief.

Sample questions have been provided on each page. Additional questions or perspectives could be applied to each word. If a word on one page doesn't work for you...pick another = Repick.

"Time does not heal all wounds. Actively working through your grief may." (Lisa Zoll)

React

Photo Credit: Leigh Ann Bryan

What was your initial reaction to the event?

Retell

Are there specific parts of your story that you tend to tell and retell?

Response

Photo Credit: Linda Jacobs

What kind of responses have you
had to the event? How do you
cope with them?

Reconcile

Have you relied on spirituality or religion to help you understand your loss? If so, in what ways?

Resilience

Where do you find your strength?

Reconstruct

Abe Jacobs

How are you rebuilding your life since the loss?

Release

Abe Jacobs

Are there aspects of the loss that you have been able to let go of?

Relinquish

What do you find most difficult to let go of?

Redo

Is there anything you would redo?

Rethink

What aspects of your life have
you re-thought in light of the
loss?

Rejoice

Are there things about your loved one's life that you have been able to celebrate?

Retreat

Photo Credit: Shannon O'Shea

Where do you go or what do you do when you need to get away from everybody and everything?

Reflect

What do you reflect on most often when you think about your loss or your loved one?

Reminisce

What are some of your fondest
memories of your loved one?

Reframe

Has the way you look at your loss changed over time?

Restore

Photo Credit: Bonnie Spease Bentz

Have you been able to restore
any part(s) of the life that
changed because of your loss?

Rebound

Are there small ways in which you
have rebounded from your loss?

Readjust

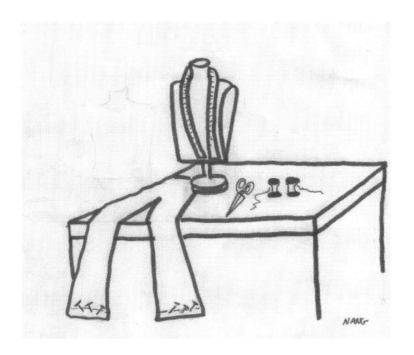

What was the most difficult
adjustment that you had to make
because of your loss? What have
you had to readjust in your life?

Renew

Do you have a renewed
perspective or passion for
anything?

Revive

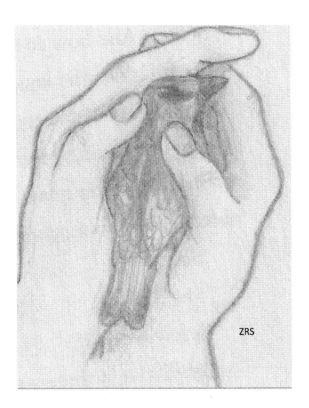

Are there any activities you did before the loss that you have stopped doing? Are there any activities you could start doing again?

Resolve

Photo Credit: Bonnie Spease Bentz

Are there any particular things you have resolved to do in light of your loss?

Remember

Jen and Dave

What do you do to remember
your loved ones on their
birthdays, holidays, and special
occasions?

Relive

Photo Credit: Michelle Smey

What events do you relive most often? Happy, sad, or both?

Re-engage

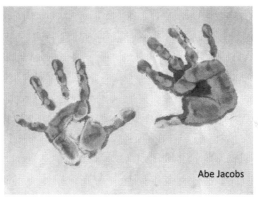

Abe Jacobs

What are some activities you see yourself getting involved in to help you deal with your loss?

Repair

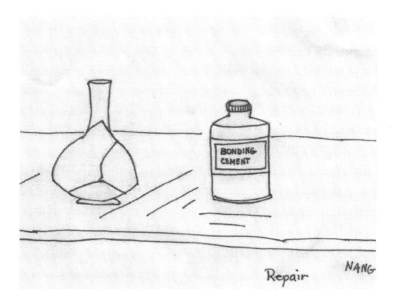

Repair   NANG

Are there any relationships that
are in need of repair?

Relief

Photo Credit: Lorie Shaull

Did you experience any relief since your loss?

Re-examine

Photo Credit: Bonnie Spease Bentz

Are there parts of your life, past or present, that you have found yourself examining or re-examining?

Reasons

? ? W ? ?

? WHY ?

? ? Y ? ?

Do you seek answers to this
question? Have you found any?
What are the most frequent
questions you ask?

Reconnect

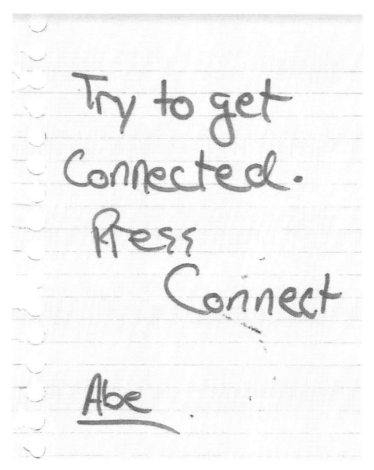

Are there people you have reconnected with or people you would like to reconnect with since your loss?

Remorse

Are there things you wish you would have done differently or could change? Were there words left unsaid?

Relax

What are some activities or
thoughts that relax you?

Rebel

Are there ways in which you have acted out because of your loss?

Reach

Photo Credit: Lynn Shiner

To whom can you reach out for support?

Reaffirm

Photo Credit: Lisa Zoll

What have you experienced that has been life-affirming? What in your life gives you strength?

Religion

Are there ways in which religion
has been helpful or hurtful?

Realign

Photo Credit: Shannon O'Shea

How have you realigned your priorities?

Realize

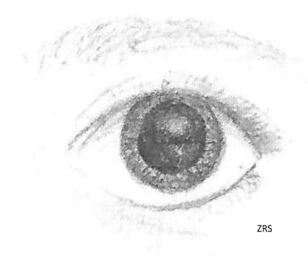

ZRS

Have you learned anything about yourself as a result of the loss?

Ready

Photo Credit: Lorie Shaull

What are you ready to do? Are there things that you are not ready to do?

Receive

Kelsey Bentz

What kind of support have you received? From whom? Have you found it difficult to ask for help?

Refocus

Photo Credit: Linda Jacobs

What do you focus on now that you didn't focus on before?

Recreate

Photo Credit: Linda Jacobs

In what ways are you recreating your life, hopes, and dreams?

Re-cultivate

Have you resumed any of your hobbies or interests? Have you found any new interests?

Read

Photo Credit: Bob Monk

Have you read books, poems,
scriptures, etc. that have been
helpful? If so, what were they?

Resist

Are there people, places, and/or things you avoid?

Re-emerge

Photo Credit: Bonnie Spease Bentz

How would you like to see
yourself emerge from this
experience?

Reject

Photo Credit: Lynn Shiner

To whom or what do you find yourself saying "no"?

Reclaim

Photo Credit: Linda Jacobs

What in your life have you reclaimed or do you want to reclaim?

Rely

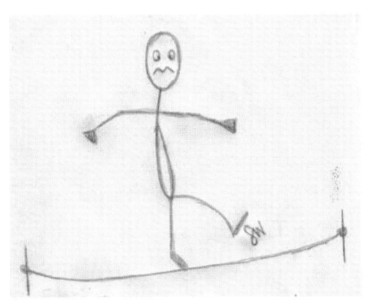

Trusting others to respect your individual grief process is like walking a tightrope and relying on something higher to protect you. (Shannon Wood)

Who can you rely on? Are there different people you rely on for different things?

Recognize

What have you learned to recognize about yourself?

Notes and Reflections

_____

_____

_____

_____

_____

_____

_____

_____

_____

_____

_____

_____

_____

_____

Part IV: Supporting the Griever

"Let's face it, *death is awkward.* Most people, even with the best of intentions, are often out of their comfort zone."
(Lynn Shiner)

David

Supporting the Griever – Advice from Lynn

We live in a society where others shy away from their worst nightmare. If the nightmare happened to you, then it could happen to them. People don't want to be reminded that such tragedies occur. Most people, even with the best of intentions, are often out of their comfort zone. Let's face it, death is awkward and sometimes it's just easier to avoid.

I believe the unwillingness is not because people don't care or don't want to help, I truly believe that we are not always certain what the right thing is to say or do, or we have a fear that we may hurt the person even more.

For any of us who support, interact with those who have lost a loved one to violence, or for that matter any type death, my best advice, remember your ABC's:

A - Avoid Clichés
B - Be a Good Listener
C - Converse

A – Avoid Clichés: For me personally, some of the well-meaning comments said by friends, family and co-workers:

- "Time heals all wounds."
- "Didn't you see this coming?"
- "I know how you feel, my grandmother died."
- "At least they were young; if they were older you would have been more attached to them."
- "Be thankful, you can have more children."
- "It could have been worse."
- "It was God's will."
- "God never gives us more than we can handle."
- "They're in a better place now."
- "You have to just let it go and move on."
- "Everything happens for a reason."

For most, there is no comfort in these statements. If a sentence is forming in our mind and it starts with "at least" or "be thankful," we need to bite our tongue.

Let's go back. "It was God's will?" When a pastor said that to me, I looked at him as though he was nuts. I don't think that God picked Jen and Dave and said, "Their father will stab them 10 times and then take his own life."

"Everything happens for a reason?" No. It doesn't. Sometimes the most horrific unimaginable things happen to good people. And sometimes, life is cruel and doesn't make sense.

And, when we tell someone to "move on or get over it," that's like telling a blind person to look a little closer.

We really need to be careful with our choice of words.

When we don't know what to say but feel the need to say something, we should use simple words:
- "I'm sorry."
- "I'm sorry this happened to you. I can't imagine what you are going through."

- "It breaks my heart to see you suffering."
- "This is so unfair."
- "I'm really at a loss for words. I just want you to know I care and have been thinking about you."

A small gesture to show that you care.

B - Be Willing to Listen: If you want to support those whose loved ones have died, it is important to remember that the greatest comfort comes from actively listening without judgment, acknowledging their pain, their fears, and creating an atmosphere that gives permission for them to feel whatever they are feeling at the moment, and to express even the most outrageous feelings. Remember, our job is not to fix them or make sense of what happened. We simply need to be present, validate their feelings, be willing to feel a little awkward, and have an open and listening heart. This is an amazing gift than can make a difference.

C - Converse: Talk about the person who died. Those remaining like to be asked about their loved ones. They often like to describe

their loved ones and share fond memories.
Don't be afraid to mention their name. If
you knew the deceased personally, share a
memory. It won't remind the person of their
loss. Trust me, they haven't forgotten.

Grief is a strange thing.

"Death's greatest power is not that it can make people die, but that it can make people left behind want to stop living" (Backman, 2015).

"Each person's grief is like *all* other people's grief; each person's grief is like *some* other people's grief; and each person's grief is like *no* other person's grief" (Worden, 2008).

"Mourning has no timetable. Grief is not the same for everybody. And it does not always go away. The closest one can find to a consensus about it among today's therapists is the conviction that the healthiest way to deal with it is to lean into it, rather than to keep it at bay" (Epstein, 2013).

"Grief is a jerk" (Blooms, 2017).

Why We Dance
To dance is to pray,
To pray is to heal,
To heal is to give,
To give is to live,
To live is to dance.
-Marijo Moore

Photo Credit:
Lorie Shaull at the Prairie
Island & Wacipi/Pow Wow
in Mendota, MN

Appendix

A Grief Trajectory

By Lisa S. Zoll, LCSW & Lynn Shiner

According to Fredrik Backman in *A Man Called Ove*, death is a strange thing. It is also perplexing, puzzling, and mysterious. It is a unique and unpredictable process for each person, and responses are highly personal. There have been scholarly attempts to put the process into stages, states, and tasks. While these efforts provide a roadmap for clinicians who treat individuals experiencing grief, there is little that can be done to harness the grieving process into a straight path that can easily be followed by those who grieve.

There are multiple definitions of grief that range from simplistic to complex. In *Treatment of Complicated Mourning,* Therese A. Rando defines grief as "the process of experiencing the psychological, behavioral, social and physical reactions to the perception of loss." A more complex definition suggests that grief is a multifaceted response to loss, particularly to the loss of someone or something that has died, where a bond or affection was involved. Although conventionally focused on the emotional response to loss, grief also, according to Vuurden Psychology, has physical, cognitive, behavioral, social, spiritual, and philosophical dimensions.

The definition of grief that will be used in this article is that grief is a response to the loss of someone, something, or somewhere where a significant and emotional bond has been formed. This may include a tragic death, a divorce, a loss of a job, or a move from a beloved home.

Regardless of the definition, common reactions to grief include, but are not limited to, sadness; longing; missing the deceased; nonacceptance of the death; feeling the death was unfair; anger; feeling stunned, dazed, or shocked; emptiness; preoccupation with thoughts and images of the deceased; loss of enjoyment; difficulties in trusting others; social impairments; and guilt concerning the circumstances of the death.

Many scholars of thanatology have proposed that grief can be put into linear stages, that there are specific tasks that one must complete, or that there is a predetermined process to grieving. More recently, the transtheoretical model of change—encompassing emotions, attitudes, intentions, behavioral processes, regression, and maintenance—has been applied to the process of grief. While these approaches attempt to define the experience and process of grief, there are shortcomings to any model that tries to make grief an orderly and definitive process or experience. Therefore, a new model, comprising event grief, working grief, and forever grief, will be explored as a possible trajectory of grief. No timeframe is imposed on achieving these stages.

Case Illustration: A Woman's Experience Through the Trajectory

Lynn Shiner experienced a tragic and traumatic loss when her ex-husband murdered her two children, Jen and Dave, on Christmas Eve 1994. In her book, ***Stabbed in the Heart: Three Murdered Children, Two Resilient Mothers***, she tells the story of her grief event that began 23 years ago, the work of grief that she has done, and her forever grief, which she continues to live with today and will continue to live with in the future. She found it difficult to place herself in any stage of grief, to find any form of closure as it related to the loss of her children, or to fit her experience into any model that was presented to her in her grief counseling. She believed that she was not meeting the expectations of the parameters set by clinical models, resulting in additional feelings of anxiety and inadequacy. Shiner believed that her experience could best be expressed in a trajectory: the event, the work, and the never-ending process of grieving the loss, thus removing stages, expectations, order, and timeframes.

The Event Grief

Their father stabbed Jen, 10, and Dave, 8, to death. Shiner's response to this discovery resulted in an initial physiological reaction that included numbness, vomiting, wailing, racing heart, chest pains, and uncontrollable shaking. In the days that followed, she experienced suicidal thoughts along with an intense yearning to be with her children. She existed in a "zombielike" state where she experienced panic attacks, anxiety, confusion, fear, and a complete loss of control of daily life. Grief stripped away her independence, beliefs, confidence, self-esteem, and hope, leaving her vulnerable, exposed, and dependent on others. She felt incapable of decision making. The visions of the event and memories of her children were overwhelming; the "what-ifs" were endless.

The Work of Grief

In the beginning, grief controls the griever; over time the griever begins to have some control over the grief by doing the hard work of grieving. It is an engaging process in which the griever must actively participate. After the initial event, Shiner was stripped of her life as she knew it. She began to move forward slowly with the support of her boyfriend, who listened to her telling and retelling the story daily in all its painful aspects and who helped to keep her from ending her life. She returned to her job after three weeks to provide some routine and structure to her life, even though her ability to fulfill her role was compromised. She began seeing a psychologist twice a week. She surrounded herself with a small support system of people whom she knew that she could trust, assessing each person based on whether she felt safe with them. Additional work involved coming to terms with her spirituality, asking, "Why would God allow something like this to occur?"

The work of grief in Shiner's case involved keeping the deceased in her life, talking about them, talking to them, sensing their presence, and deciding how her relationship with them would continue. In searching for meaning in her loss, she became an advocate for children and crime victims, spending most of her career strengthening legislation, technology, and policies that would support victim services, including the passage of the Jen and Dave Law. Initially, her motivation for her work was her own survival, not realizing the impact that her efforts would have on others. The work that she was doing would ultimately rebuild what was stripped away from her by tragic loss.

The Forever Grief

Shiner's grief work continues into this aspect of the trajectory. While she has periodically experienced upsurges of her grief (e.g., Christmas, Mother's Day, birthdays, graduations, and weddings) the intensity and duration of the feelings are diminished and the grief no longer consumes or controls her life as it did in the previous stages of grief.

With Nancy Chavez, she coauthored *Stabbed in the Heart*, a book that describes her experience from the event grief to the forever grief. The book became a way for her to, not only memorialize her children and describe the important role of community, but to share her journey of resilience, endurance, and life beyond the loss of Jen and Dave. Her memories of her children have become fond and comforting rather than painful and have given her a sense of joy and hope. Shiner has discovered that grief is the scholar of life, its teachings are immeasurable, and it is a powerful reminder of how fragile life can be.

Approaches to Grief

The trajectory of grief seeks to explore the experience of grief in a less structured way as identified in the stages or tasks often associated with grief. It is meant to be fluid in nature with work being done throughout the trajectory. The first aspect of the trajectory is the event grief itself. This includes the event that causes an individual to have an emotional reaction to a loss. It is loss that held significance and to which an attachment was formed. In Shiner's case, it was the murder of her two children.

The work of grief comes in many forms. In *Grief Counselling and Grief Therapy: A Handbook for the Mental Health Practitioner*, J. William Worden illustrates the following tasks that the grieving individual should complete to accommodate the loss:

- accept the reality of the loss;
- experience the pain of the loss;
- adjust to the environment without the person, place, or thing; and
- reinvest in a new reality.

Robert A. Neimeyer, PhD, approaches grieving from a constructivist approach. ***In Lessons of Loss: A Guide to Coping***, he suggests that "Meaning reconstruction in response to a loss is the central process of grieving." The constructivist approach uses cognitive processes to emphasize sense-making and benefit-finding within the grieving process. Cognitive behavioral therapy has been utilized to help alleviate symptoms of grief by helping the bereaved to work on changing irrational beliefs and thoughts into rational beliefs and thoughts. According to Ruth Malkinson, PhD, the hard work of grief is multifaceted and can involve any combination of these and other evidenced-based approaches since no two individuals grieve in the same way.

Part of the ongoing work of grief is finding ways to cope with what Rando described as a sudden temporary upsurge of grief (STUG). These events produce a reaction with periods of intense grief that occur when a catalyst reminds one of the absence of the loved one or resurrects memories of the death, the loved one, or feelings about the loss. These reactions can be expected and can happen in response to anniversaries, birthdays, and family celebrations. Or, they can be unexpected in

113

the form of a song on the radio, a smell, or something that is read or seen that brings up the memory of a loss. They tend to catch the individual off guard and, according to the Open to Hope website, "come like a bolt out of the blue. Those intense upsurges of grief that take you totally by surprise. They ambush you, triggering an up bubble of grief emotions."

The approach taken depends upon the individual's experience of loss and how that individual finds ways to accommodate or assimilate the loss into their lives, either on their own or with the assistance of a therapist, counselor, clergy, support group, family, and/or friends. The assumption is that, regardless of the approach, grieving is an ongoing process that leads to some level of adaptation at some point in the process, and the individual moves from doing the hard work of grief to forever grief in the trajectory. The transition is most likely to occur when the event no longer controls or consumes the griever's life. Shiner made this realization 10 to 13 years after the event and this indicated to her that she was moving forward in the trajectory. She believes that without the work it would be difficult for grievers to move forward.

Forever grief is the grief that will linger in various forms long after the loss and involves coping with reminders that bring stored memories to consciousness. Residual forms of grief such as STUGs remain in the forever grief, with the duration and intensity diminished. According to the Mayo Clinic, when you lose someone close, your grief doesn't just magically end in time; reminders often bring back the pain of the loss. Additionally, as time goes on, fond memories surface and can become a source of comfort, peace, and joy to the griever. Individuals learn how to cope and find ways to weave their loss into a new life that has been forged through their grief work. In this way, grief becomes an opportunity for growth rather than an obstacle to living. For Shiner, living with grief has become the trajectory of her life. Her work will go on in ways that help her to make meaning and find benefit in her loss.

While the trajectory of grief does not offer exact stages for individuals to pass through or tasks for individuals to accomplish, it demonstrates a trajectory that individuals can be expected to experience following a grief event. It postulates that grieving a loss may never come to a definitive end and that closure is a myth. It does not mean that an individual cannot and will not return to a meaningful life by finding ways to accept the reality of the loss as suggested by the tasks of grief suggested by Worden, by constructing meaning in the meaning reconstruction approach of Neimeyer, or by working to alter irrational thought patterns as suggested by Malkinson. This trajectory can serve as a path that begins at the grief event and moves through the twists and turns of the grief experience.

Reprinted with the permission of Social Work Today ©. Great Valley Publishing, Co.

ABOUT THE AUTHORS

Lisa Zoll graduated with her MSW from Temple University, Harrisburg in 2003. Lisa's experience includes 12 years as a Clinical Psychiatric Specialist at the Penn State University Medical Center in Hershey, Pennsylvania, working in the Adult Partial Hospitalization Program and Psychiatric Outpatient Clinic. In 2008, Lisa began teaching "Loss & Grief" and "Assessment and the DSM" as an Adjunct Instructor in the School of Social Work at Temple University, Harrisburg. In 2014 she was hired as a full-time instructor in the Master of Social Work program where she continues teaching courses on grief, loss, and clinical assessment.

Lynn Shiner dedicated most of her career to supporting crime victims. This work grew out of Lynn's very personal experience of tragic loss. On Christmas Day, 1994, Lynn's young children, Jen and Dave, were murdered. Later, as the Director of the Pennsylvania Office of Victims' Services, Lynn oversaw the annual distribution of more than one hundred million dollars in state and federal funding allocated to meet the needs of crime victims throughout the Commonwealth. She is the recipient of countless awards including the "National Crime Victim Service Award" presented by John Ashcroft. Lynn retired from the Commonwealth after 37 years of service and is now offering her expertise as an independent consultant.

Lisa Zoll

Lynn Shiner